Designer   David West
Art Director   Charles Matheson
Editor   James McCarter
Researcher   Dee Robinson
Consultant   C. C. Horton

Illustrators   James G. Robins
           Hayward Art Group

First published in Great Britain in 1983 by
William Collins Sons & Co Ltd

First published in the United States in 1983 by
Gloucester Press

Copyright © Aladdin Books Ltd 1983

Printed in Belgium

ISBN 0-531-03463-1

Library of Congress Catalog
Card Number: 82-84452

Contents

The Inside Story

NUCLEAR SUBMARINE

Mike Rossiter

GLOUCESTER PRESS
NEW YORK · TORONTO · 1983

Killer Beneath the Waves

Submarines were first built in large numbers at the beginning of this century. They proved to be deadly weapons during World War I (1914-18), sinking thousands of ships in the battle to control the North Atlantic Ocean. Thereafter, submarines were to be an essential feature in any naval conflict.

Many advances in the design of conventional, diesel-electric engined submarines were made during World War II (1939-45) and after, but the development of nuclear power was a gigantic step forward. Diesel-electric submarines need to come to the surface of the ocean, to replenish air supplies and get rid of exhaust gases. With nuclear power, the only limit on how long a submarine can remain submerged is the endurance of its crew.

Nuclear submarines are in service in the navies of the U.S., the U.K., France, China and the Soviet Union. There are two types, the hunter/killer, or attack, submarine and the missile-carrying submarine, or SSBN. Hunter/killers are designed to attack other submarines and enemy vessels – the traditional job of a submarine in war. The SSBN is a wholly new and frightening weapon. Its role is to serve as a moving platform for nuclear missiles, hidden somewhere in the depths of the ocean. The world's SSBN forces threaten certain retaliation to any country that makes first use of nuclear weapons, a threat designed to prevent the outbreak of a future war.

Nuclear submarines are highly complex pieces of machinery, and cost enormous amounts of money to build, with construction (1) lasting for four years or more. After its official launch (2), the sub undergoes extensive sea trials (3), testing every piece of equipment for performance and reliability, before it receives its crew and is commissioned into service (4). On active service, tours of duty may last as long as three months (5). Modern nuclear subs have an operational life of about seven years before they need a major refit in dry dock (6).

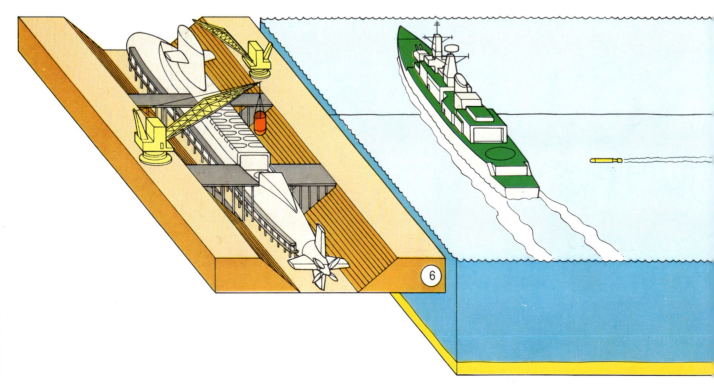

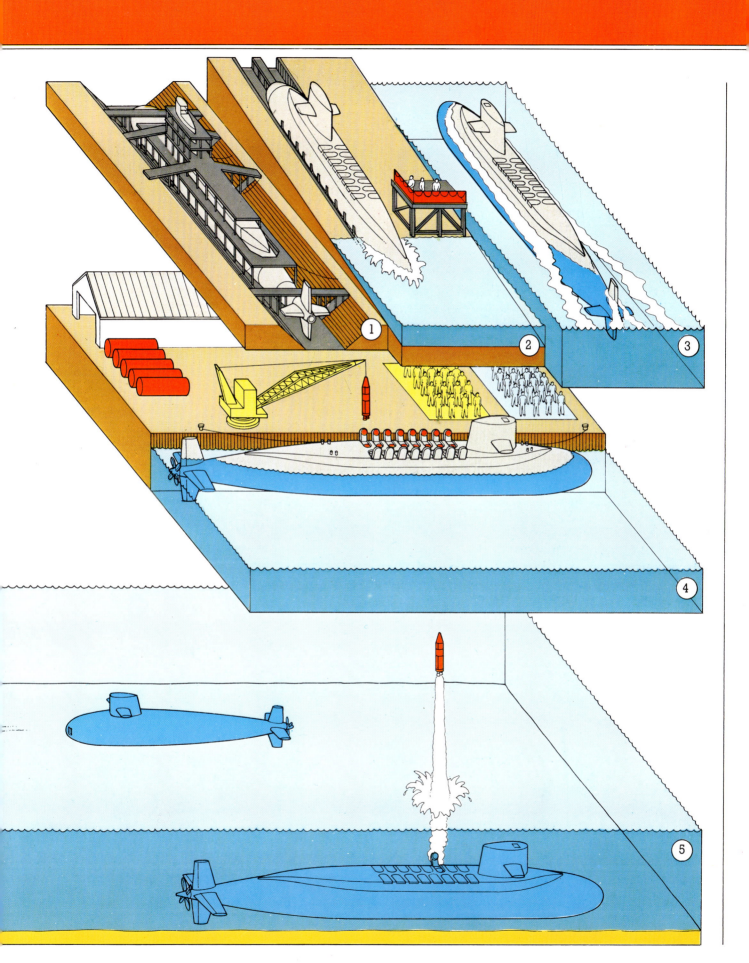

"Under Way on Nuclear Power"

The first nuclear submarine – in fact, the first vessel of any kind to use nuclear power – was the USS *Nautilus*. At the time of her launch, January 1954, *Nautilus* was the world's largest submarine. Almost exactly a year later, she flashed an historic message from Long Island Sound, a stretch of water off the eastern coast of the U.S.: "Under way on nuclear power."

In the years that followed, *Nautilus* and her successors – *Seawolf*, *Skate*, *Swordfish*, *Sargo*, and *Snapdragon* – rapidly demonstrated the tremendous advantages that nuclear power gives a submarine. In 1958, *Nautilus* passed across the North Pole, sailing deep beneath the thick polar icecap, showing that there was no ocean in the world that a submarine could not command. In the same year, *Seawolf* made a record dive lasting 60 days, a duration that is now common. A year later, USS *Skate* surfaced at the North Pole, breaking through the polar ice.

Away from the Arctic Ocean, the USS *Triton*, the first nuclear submarine to have two nuclear reactors, was also breaking records. In 1960 she completed an incredible submerged voyage around the world, covering 57,930 km (36,000 miles) in 84 days.

These new submarines, capable of prolonged submergence at depths of over 200 m (656 ft) and speeds of more than 48 km/h (30 miles/h), were formidable attack vessels. But one further development – the ability to fire long-range missiles from beneath the ocean – completely changed the nature of undersea warfare. The first submarine-launched missile was fired in July 1960, from the USS *George Washington*. The missile was called Polaris, and could be armed with a nuclear warhead capable of destroying an entire city. One of the most sinister weapons the world has ever seen, the missile-carrying nuclear submarine, had arrived.

USS *Nautilus* beneath the polar ice.

The first-ever nuclear submarine, USS *Nautilus*, made many voyages beneath the polar icecap. Launched in 1954, her nuclear fuel did not need replacing until 1957, after the *Nautilus* had sailed over 111,000 km (69,000 miles). *Nautilus* was 91 m (300 ft) long and weighed over 2,950 tonnes (2,900 tons) when submerged. The largest of today's submarines are nearly twice that length and weigh six times as much.

The powertrain

The energy generated in the reactor creates steam which turns a series of turbines. These are connected to the propeller by a drive shaft and gears. Great effort is spent to make the submarine run as quietly as possible to avoid detection by enemy ships.

Missiles

At the center of the submarine, to the rear of the fin, is a raised section of the hull that holds two lines of vertically mounted missile launch tubes. The size of an SSBN is dictated by the size and number of the missiles it is designed to carry.

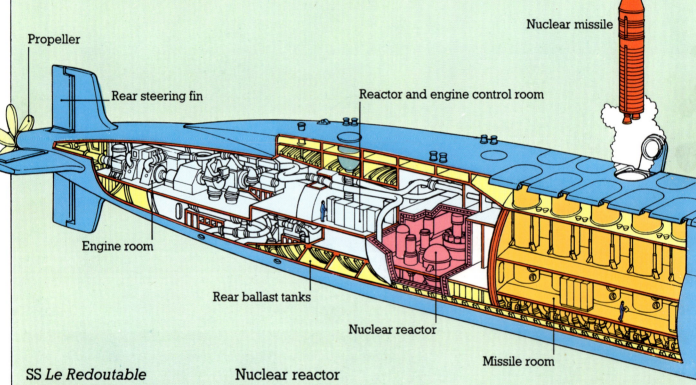

Propeller

Rear steering fin

Reactor and engine control room

Nuclear missile

Engine room

Rear ballast tanks

Nuclear reactor

Missile room

SS *Le Redoutable*

The SS *Le Redoutable*, shown here, launched in 1967, was France's first SSBN. It has all the basic equipment typically found in missile-carrying submarines. Attack submarines are smaller, and do not have missile launch tubes. In attack subs, torpedo tubes can be positioned at the front, rear and middle of the hull.

Nuclear reactor

The nuclear reactor is fueled by a small piece of uranium. This gives off harmful radiation, so the reactor has a thick lead shield to protect the crew. The reactor also needs constant cooling, to stop it from over-heating. As well as powering the boat, the reactor is the source of all the electricity used on board the sub.

The Fin, or Sail

The fin, or sail, acts as a bridge when the sub has surfaced and contains the submarine's aerials, snorkels, periscopes and other equipment. Hydroplanes attached to the side help keep the sub stable when submerged.

Living Quarters

Beneath the fin are the crew's quarters, officers' wardrooms, storerooms, galleys and the operations and communications center of the sub. With crews of up to 140 men, great care is taken to provide recreation and comfort for long voyages.

Hull and bows

A submarine has an inner and outer hull. Between the two are ballast tanks which are flooded with water when the submarine dives. In order to withstand high water pressures when submerged, the hull is made of extra-strong steel alloys, and special welding techniques are used in construction. The bow contains torpedo launch tubes, used to defend the boat should it come under attack by an enemy submarine. This is also where the main sonar detection equipment is housed.

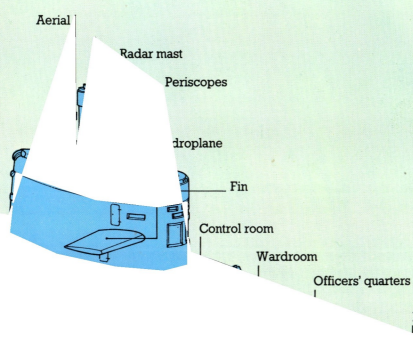

Aerial

Radar mast

Periscopes

droplane

Fin

Control room

Wardroom

Officers' quarters

Forward escape hatch

Torpedo room

Crew's quarters

Storeroom

Galley

Inner hull

Forward ballast tanks

Torpedo tubes

Modern Nuclear Submarines

Shown here are the massive USS *Ohio*, the latest missile-carrying submarine to be built for the U.S. Navy, and the USS *Jacksonville*, an attack submarine of the Los Angeles class, launched in 1978. Modern attack submarines can cost over a *billion* dollars to construct and equip, while missile-carrying submarines are even more expensive.

In the darkness of deep ocean, sound is what submarines rely upon for detection. Both types of submarines are designed to run as quietly as possible, so that they can avoid being detected by enemy ships, but for a missile-carrying submarine silence is absolutely essential.

The USS *Ohio* is 560 m (1,837 ft) long and weighs over 18,400 tonnes (18,110 tons) when submerged. In 1980 the Soviet Union launched the first of its Typhoon class missile submarines. Weighing about 30,000 tonnes (29,528 tons) it is the world's largest sub.

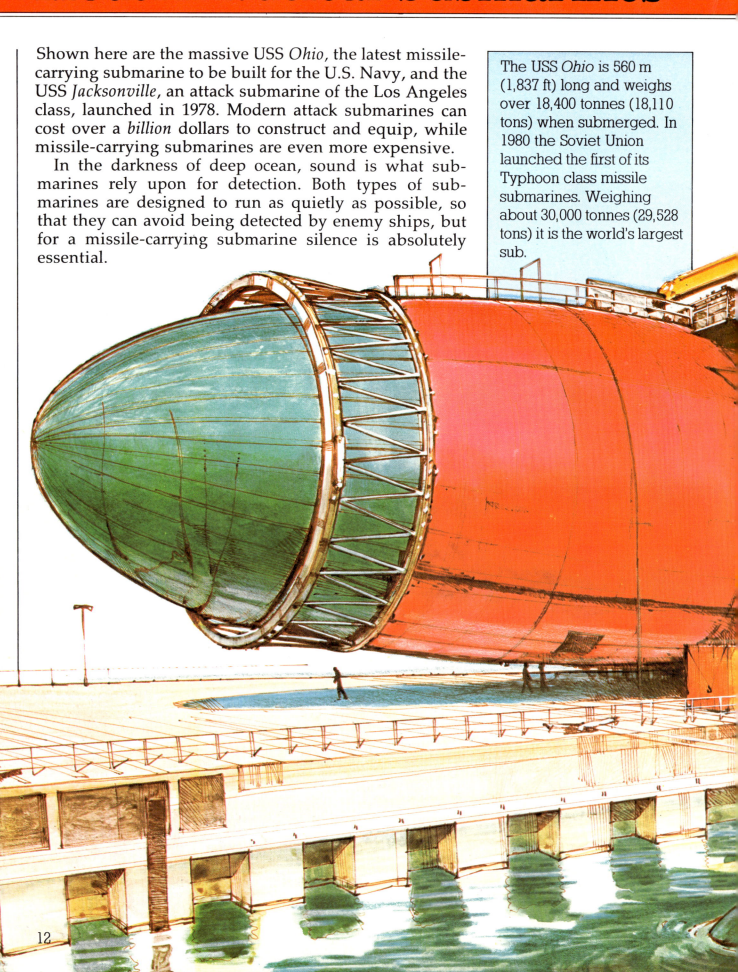

USS *Ohio* nearing completion and USS *Jacksonville* in dock.

Nuclear reactors are in themselves silent generators of power. But noise can be created by the pumps which form its cooling system, and by the turbines that the reactor powers. To keep this to a minimum, much of this equipment is mounted on beds of sound-absorbent rubber. The turbine can also be connected to run an electric motor which in turn drives the propeller, in the event of failure of the main propulsion machinery.

Countries tend not to publish exact performance figures for their submarines – they like to keep potential enemies guessing as much as possible. Los Angeles class submarines, for example, have a submerged speed of more than 48 km/h (30 miles/h), and can dive to a depth of about 450 m (1,475 ft) according to official figures, but some experts believe that in reality they are capable of 80 km/h (50 miles/h) and depths of 610 m (2,000 ft).

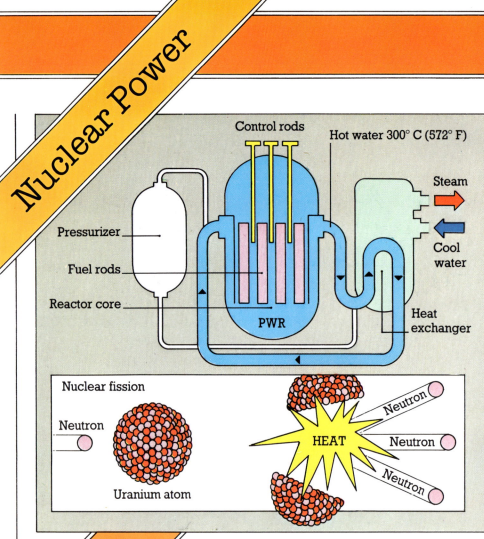

Control rods

Hot water 300° C (572° F)

Steam

Cool water

Pressurizer

Fuel rods

Reactor core

PWR

Heat exchanger

Nuclear fission

Neutron

Uranium atom

HEAT

Neutron

Neutron

Neutron

Nuclear submarines use pressurized water reactors (PWRs). These produce energy by nuclear fission. Uranium atoms in the fuel rods are unstable, and split in two, releasing three neutrons and a great deal of heat. The neutrons hit other atoms, causing them to split and so continue the reaction. Pressurized water from the pressurizer is superheated in the reactor core to about 300°C (572°F), and passed to a heat exchanger where it creates steam to power the turbines. Control rods lowered into the reactor can slow the reaction down to reduce power output.

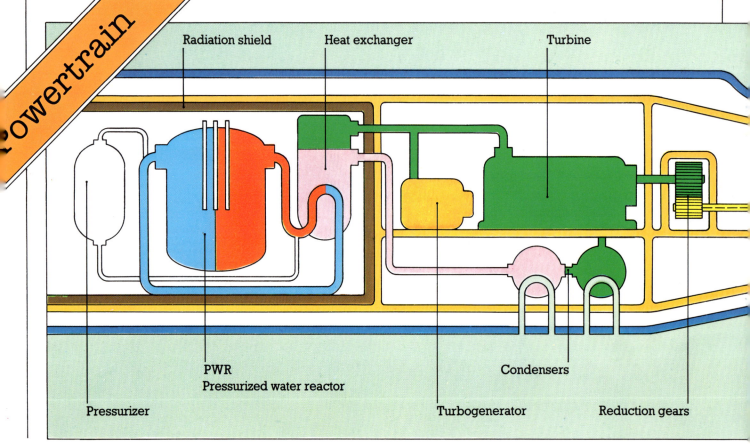

Radiation shield

Heat exchanger

Turbine

PWR
Pressurized water reactor

Condensers

Pressurizer

Turbogenerator

Reduction gears

Turbines

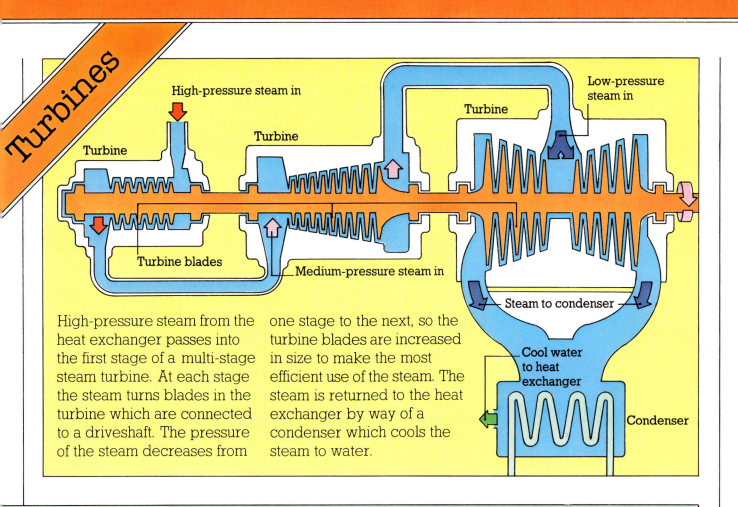

High-pressure steam in

Turbine

Turbine

Turbine

Low-pressure steam in

Turbine blades

Medium-pressure steam in

Steam to condenser

Cool water to heat exchanger

Condenser

High-pressure steam from the heat exchanger passes into the first stage of a multi-stage steam turbine. At each stage the steam turns blades in the turbine which are connected to a driveshaft. The pressure of the steam decreases from one stage to the next, so the turbine blades are increased in size to make the most efficient use of the steam. The steam is returned to the heat exchanger by way of a condenser which cools the steam to water.

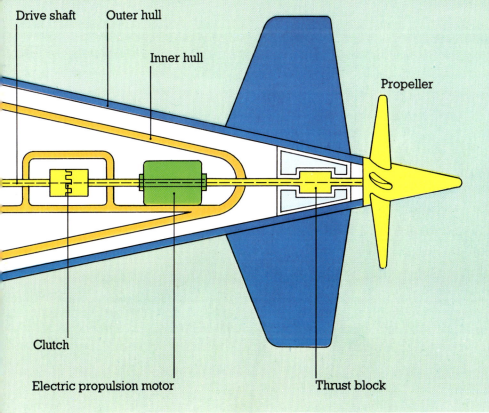

Drive shaft

Outer hull

Inner hull

Propeller

Clutch

Electric propulsion motor

Thrust block

Drive from the turbine is passed to the propeller by way of reduction gears and a clutch. The gears change the speed at which the drive shaft rotates, and the clutch simply allows the drive to be disengaged. The thrust block transmits drive from the propeller, which makes about 100 revolutions per minute. The electric motor is used only for emergency silent running. Electricity for all the sub's systems is generated in the turbogenerator, from steam from the reactor. The sub also has back-up diesel engines should the reactor fail or need to be shut down.

15

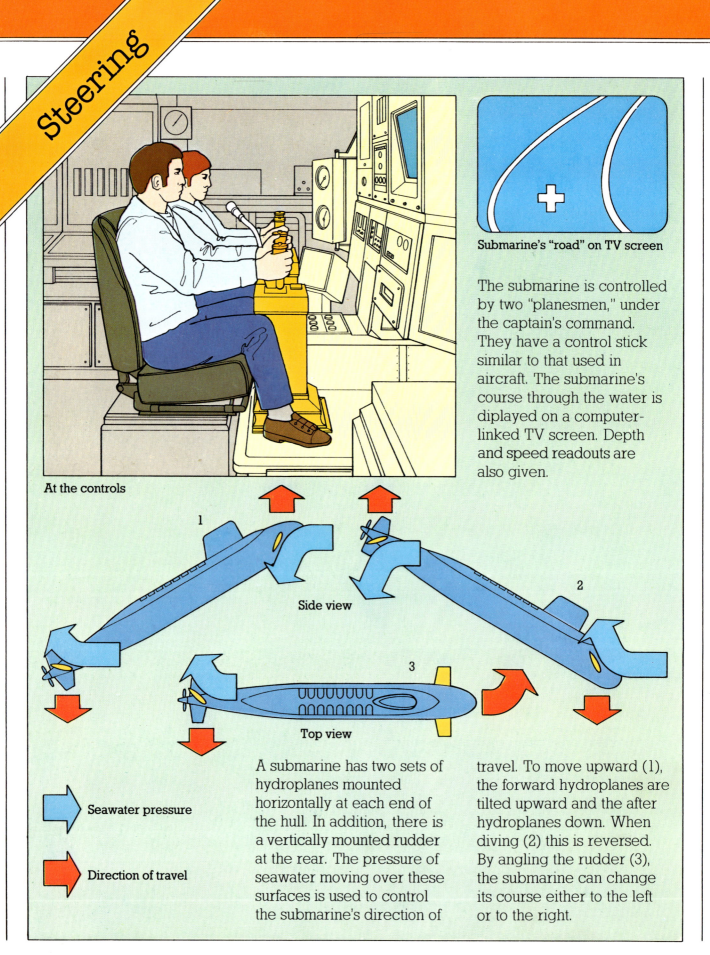

At the controls

Submarine's "road" on TV screen

The submarine is controlled by two "planesmen," under the captain's command. They have a control stick similar to that used in aircraft. The submarine's course through the water is diplayed on a computer-linked TV screen. Depth and speed readouts are also given.

Side view

Top view

Seawater pressure

Direction of travel

A submarine has two sets of hydroplanes mounted horizontally at each end of the hull. In addition, there is a vertically mounted rudder at the rear. The pressure of seawater moving over these surfaces is used to control the submarine's direction of travel. To move upward (1), the forward hydroplanes are tilted upward and the after hydroplanes down. When diving (2) this is reversed. By angling the rudder (3), the submarine can change its course either to the left or to the right.

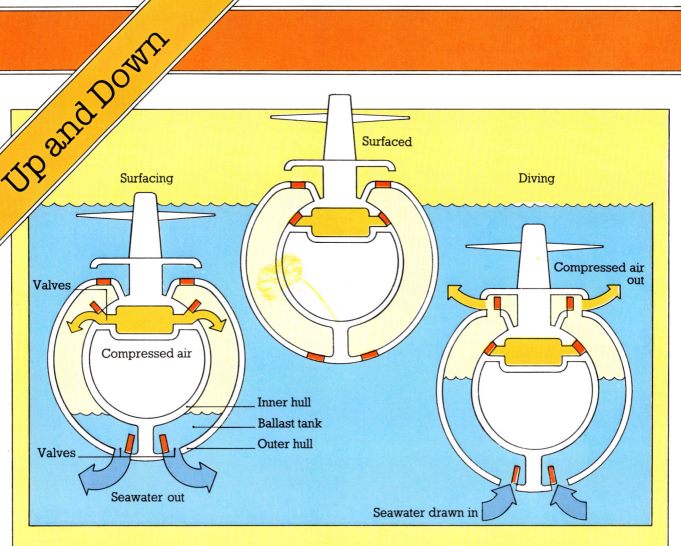

Surfacing

Surfaced

Diving

Valves

Compressed air

Valves

Inner hull

Ballast tank

Outer hull

Seawater out

Compressed air out

Seawater drawn in

Between the submarine's inner and outer hulls are ballast tanks. When the submarine is surfaced, the tanks are filled with compressed air, making the vessel buoyant. To dive, the air is released from valves at the top of the tanks and seawater rushes in at the bottom. Because the seawater is heavier than the air it displaces, the submarine sinks. To surface, the process is reversed: compressed air is fed into the tanks, forcing the seawater out, thus making the submarine lighter. Secondary tanks called trim tanks are used to compensate for weight lost when the submarine is submerged, which would otherwise unbalance the vessel. When a missile or torpedo is fired, for example, the weight lost is restored by letting an equal weight of water into the trim tanks. These trim tanks are usually controlled automatically by the submarine's computer.

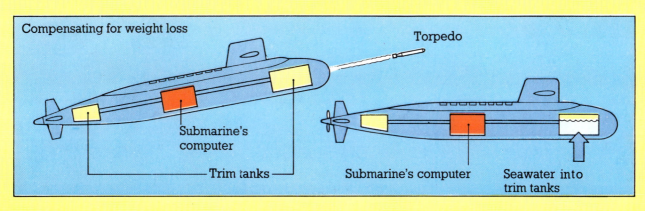

Compensating for weight loss

Torpedo

Submarine's computer

Trim tanks

Submarine's computer

Seawater into trim tanks

The Control Room

Submarines are fighting ships, and the control room is never without an air of alertness. Here, all the information that the submarine relies on to travel and survive in the ocean is brought together. The submarine's exact location at any given time can be given by the submarine's complex, computer-controlled navigation systems. A variety of listening and tracking devices will tell the submarine's commander the type, and position, of any other vessels in his vicinity, both other submarines and surface ships. Most importantly, it is from here that the submarine's weapons are fired, and instruments give an instant readout out of the state of the weapons systems.

During a patrol there will be exercises that simulate action stations. Missile-carrying subs will go through the procedures for firing their weapons; attack submarines may track enemy submarines, carry out mock battle exercises, or map areas of the ocean floor.

The crew on a nuclear submarine live close to a nuclear reactor, with the danger of exposure to harmful radiation in the unlikely event of reactor failure. Medical staff constantly monitor radiation levels, and crew members have a radiation-sensitive strip of film to warn them if any leaks occur. Under normal conditions, the environment on board is as safe as anywhere else.

The operations room at "night"

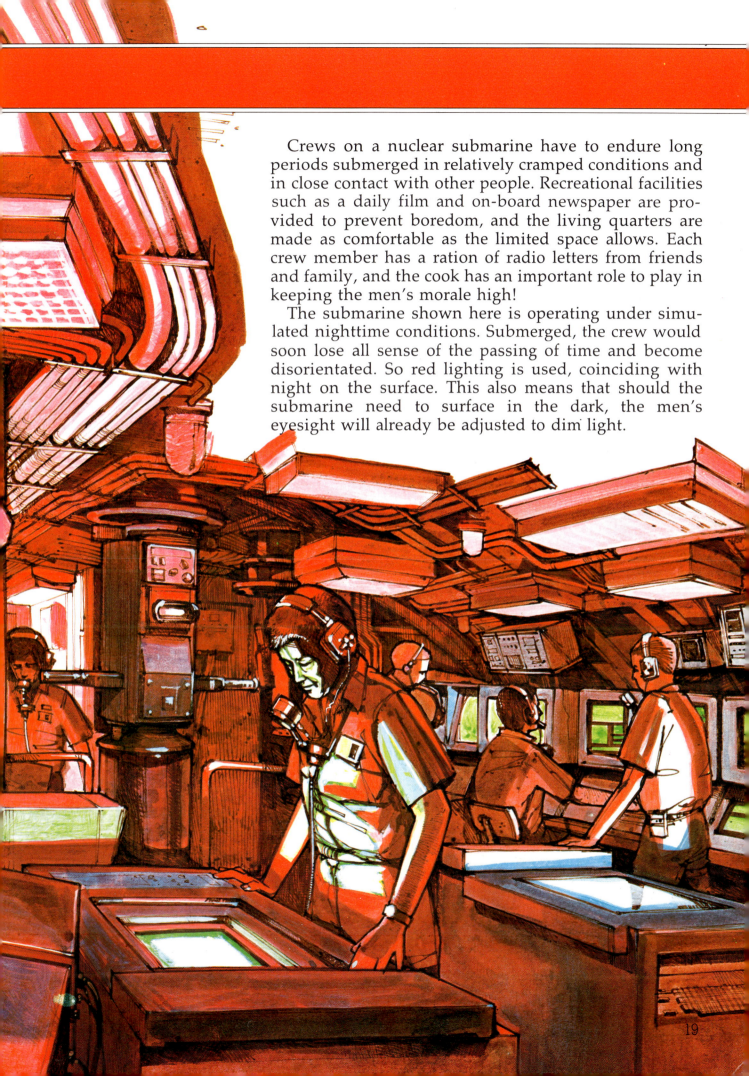

Crews on a nuclear submarine have to endure long periods submerged in relatively cramped conditions and in close contact with other people. Recreational facilities such as a daily film and on-board newspaper are provided to prevent boredom, and the living quarters are made as comfortable as the limited space allows. Each crew member has a ration of radio letters from friends and family, and the cook has an important role to play in keeping the men's morale high!

The submarine shown here is operating under simulated nighttime conditions. Submerged, the crew would soon lose all sense of the passing of time and become disorientated. So red lighting is used, coinciding with night on the surface. This also means that should the submarine need to surface in the dark, the men's eyesight will already be adjusted to dim light.

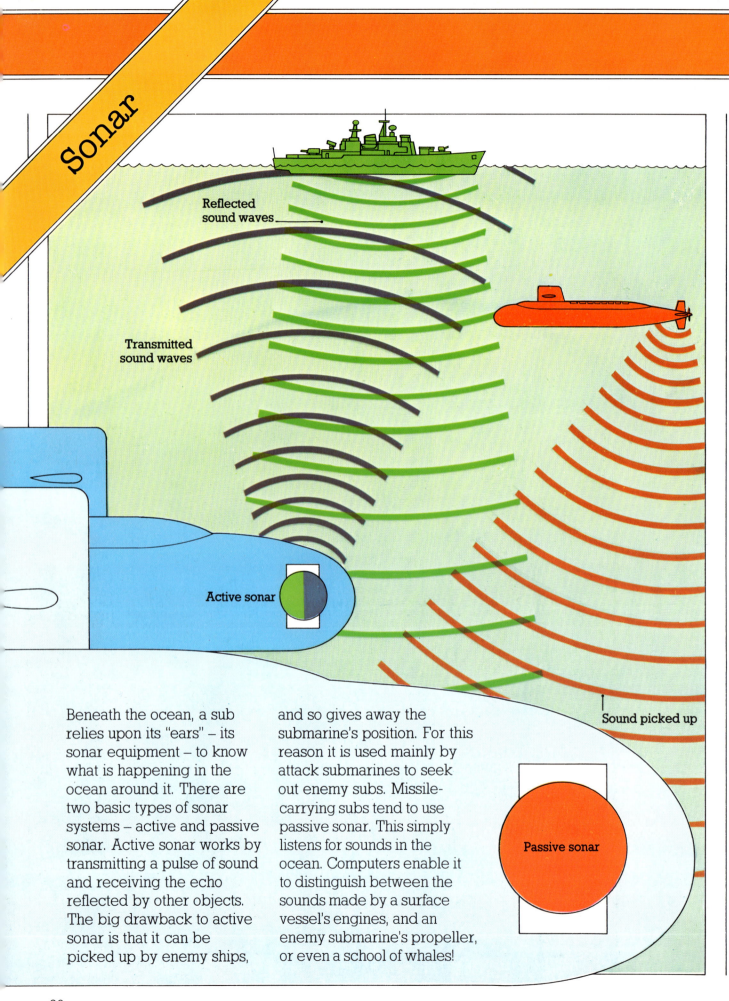

Reflected sound waves

Transmitted sound waves

Active sonar

Sound picked up

Passive sonar

Beneath the ocean, a sub relies upon its "ears" – its sonar equipment – to know what is happening in the ocean around it. There are two basic types of sonar systems – active and passive sonar. Active sonar works by transmitting a pulse of sound and receiving the echo reflected by other objects. The big drawback to active sonar is that it can be picked up by enemy ships, and so gives away the submarine's position. For this reason it is used mainly by attack submarines to seek out enemy subs. Missile-carrying subs tend to use passive sonar. This simply listens for sounds in the ocean. Computers enable it to distinguish between the sounds made by a surface vessel's engines, and an enemy submarine's propeller, or even a school of whales!

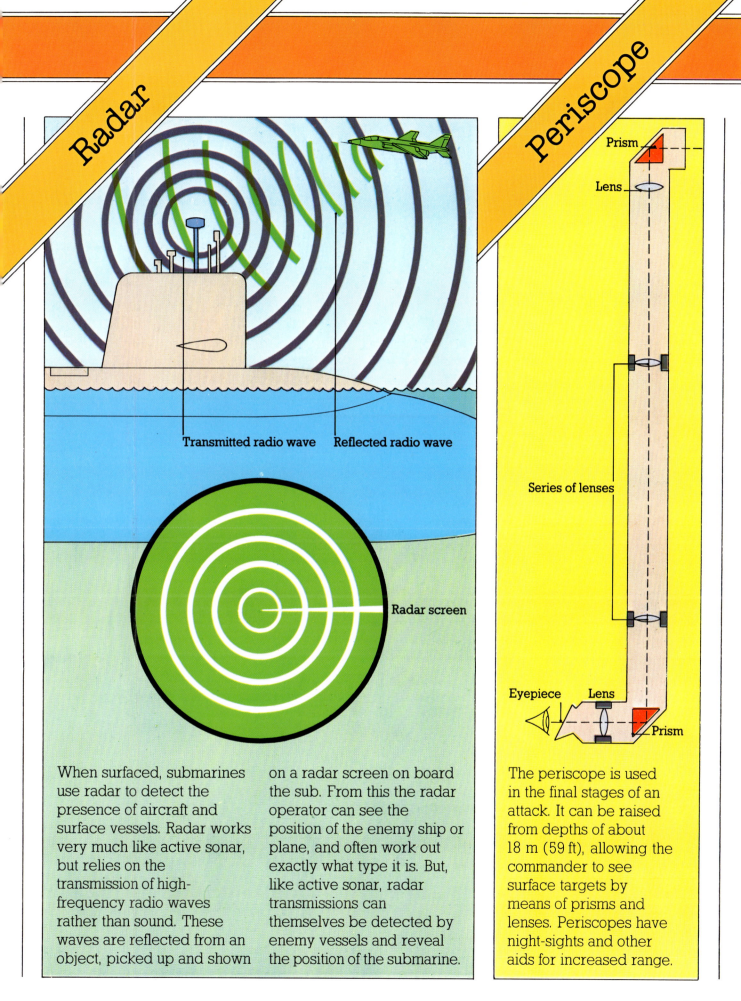

Transmitted radio wave   Reflected radio wave

Radar screen

Prism

Lens

Series of lenses

Eyepiece   Lens

Prism

When surfaced, submarines use radar to detect the presence of aircraft and surface vessels. Radar works very much like active sonar, but relies on the transmission of high-frequency radio waves rather than sound. These waves are reflected from an object, picked up and shown on a radar screen on board the sub. From this the radar operator can see the position of the enemy ship or plane, and often work out exactly what type it is. But, like active sonar, radar transmissions can themselves be detected by enemy vessels and reveal the position of the submarine.

The periscope is used in the final stages of an attack. It can be raised from depths of about 18 m (59 ft), allowing the commander to see surface targets by means of prisms and lenses. Periscopes have night-sights and other aids for increased range.

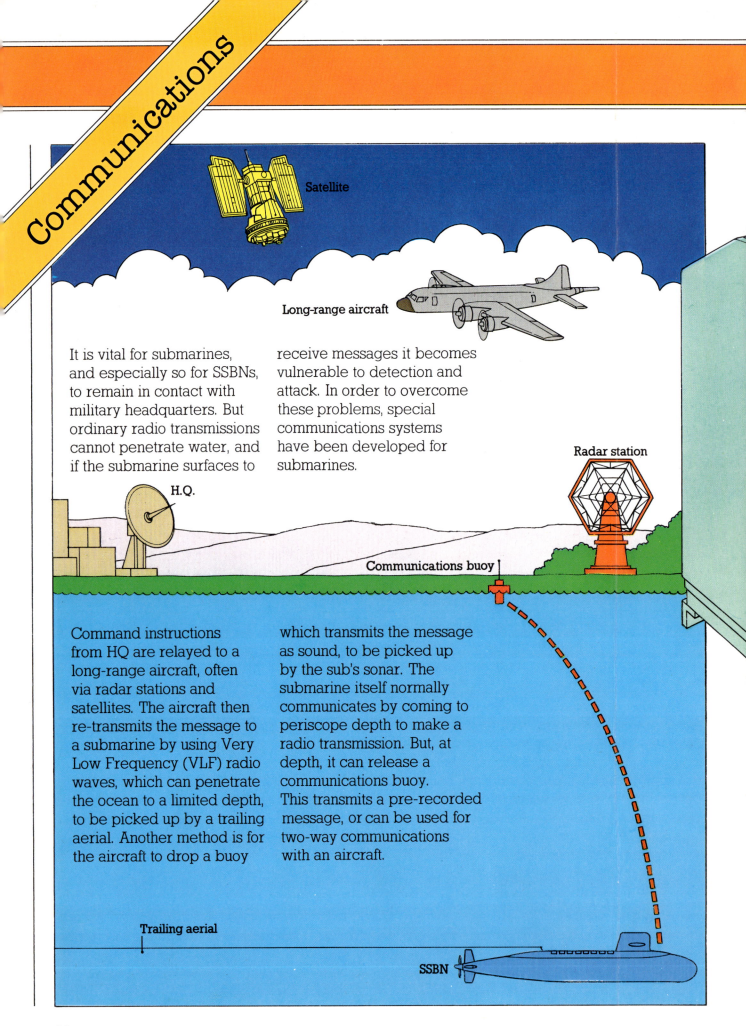

Satellite

Long-range aircraft

Radar station

H.Q.

Communications buoy

Trailing aerial

SSBN

It is vital for submarines, and especially so for SSBNs, to remain in contact with military headquarters. But ordinary radio transmissions cannot penetrate water, and if the submarine surfaces to receive messages it becomes vulnerable to detection and attack. In order to overcome these problems, special communications systems have been developed for submarines.

Command instructions from HQ are relayed to a long-range aircraft, often via radar stations and satellites. The aircraft then re-transmits the message to a submarine by using Very Low Frequency (VLF) radio waves, which can penetrate the ocean to a limited depth, to be picked up by a trailing aerial. Another method is for the aircraft to drop a buoy which transmits the message as sound, to be picked up by the sub's sonar. The submarine itself normally communicates by coming to periscope depth to make a radio transmission. But, at depth, it can release a communications buoy. This transmits a pre-recorded message, or can be used for two-way communications with an aircraft.

The submarine's sonar, radar, communications, navigation and weapons systems are all brought together in its computer, so that the captain has instant access to all aspects of his vessel's performance. The computer needs all this information too, when it is used to fire the submarine's weapons. The one shown here is able to track and engage eight different targets at once, and to control a complete attack sequence automatically.

A submarine navigates using a sophisticated, computer-controlled system called SINS (Ship's Inertial Navigation System). This monitors the submarine's exact position at any point during a voyage. Pitch, roll and yaw movements, and changes in direction and speed are automatically recorded by highly sensitive electronic equipment, and then used to plot the submarine's course relative to the starting point of its voyage. SINS is so accurate that it was correct to within 200 m (656 ft) after a voyage of over 60,000 km (37,280 miles). To obtain information about its local position, a submarine will use its active sonar and temperature probes. Active sonar can provide an accurate picture of the surface of the seabed, while the probes take readings of the temperature levels in different parts of the ocean.

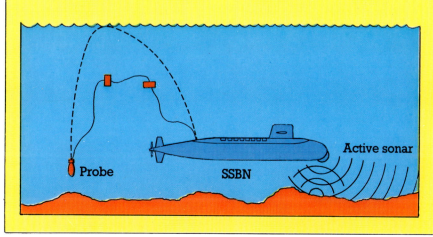

As on all naval vessels, officers and men have separate facilities. The officers' living room – called the *wardroom* – is close to the control room. The men's living room – the *mess* – can be converted into a movie theater after mealtimes. Food on submarines is of high quality, and a variety of meals are offered each day.

Sleeping

Officers and crewmen also have separate sleeping quarters. The captain has a room of his own, but junior officers may share rooms. Crewmen sleep in dormitories, where the bunks are in three tiers. These bunks can fold back into the wall, to create valuable extra space. Sleeping is arranged on a rotating basis, and each crew member has time off to relax and enjoy leisure activities.

Principle of electrolysis

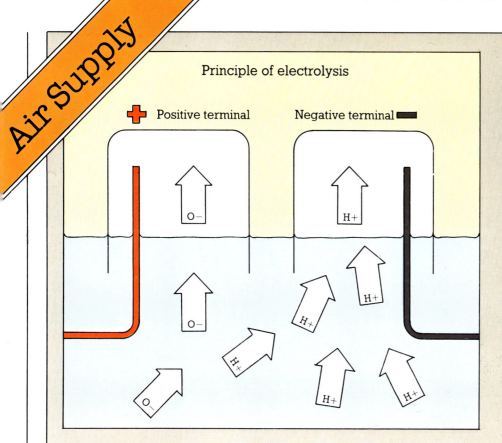

+ Positive terminal   Negative terminal **━**

O−

H+

The two most important provisions for a sub's crew are fresh air and water. The air is filtered to remove dust and carbon dioxide gas, but it must also be replenished with oxygen. This is produced by placing two charged metal plates in water and passing an electric current through it – a process known as electrolysis. The electricity splits the water molecules, freeing their oxygen and hydrogen atoms. The oxygen is collected at the positive plate and added to the air as required. Fresh water is made by distilling seawater to remove salt and other impurities.

Deep-submergence rescue vehicle

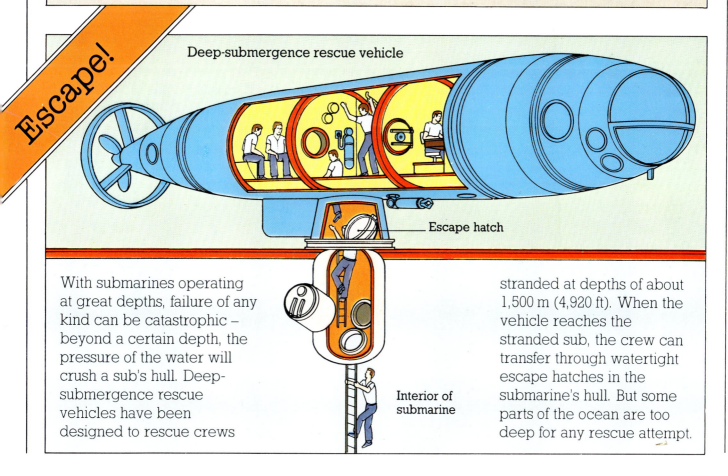

Escape hatch

Interior of submarine

With submarines operating at great depths, failure of any kind can be catastrophic – beyond a certain depth, the pressure of the water will crush a sub's hull. Deep-submergence rescue vehicles have been designed to rescue crews stranded at depths of about 1,500 m (4,920 ft). When the vehicle reaches the stranded sub, the crew can transfer through watertight escape hatches in the submarine's hull. But some parts of the ocean are too deep for any rescue attempt.

A missile-carrying submarine has two crews, called Red and Gold in the U.S. Navy, Port and Starboard in the U.K. This means that the submarine can spend the maximum amount of time at sea. When a submarine – either attack or SSBN – leaves its home base the crew on board can expect a tour of duty lasting about three months.

On leaving port, the captain gives the order to dive, and the familiar diving alarm sounds. The dive is controlled by the diving officer, who will report to the captain, "Good trim," when the submarine has reached the required depth and is under complete control.

An attack submarine will patrol a particular area of the ocean, tracking surface ships and other submarines that stray into its territory. It monitors their course and records the distinctive sonar "signature" made by their engines. Information about ocean currents and temperature layers called "thermoclines" is also recorded.

Some patrols will include naval exercises, where battle tactics and weapons systems can be tested under realistic conditions. Obviously, this is much easier for attack subs, which can use discarded vessels as targets for their missiles and torpedoes. But the crews of SSBNs must also be thoroughly familiar with their weapons routine and they regularly rehearse the firing sequence.

The USS *Guitarro* on patrol

This is the USS *Guitarro*, a Sturgeon class attack submarine in service with the Pacific Fleet. It is armed with antisubmarine torpedoes, Subrock antisubmarine missiles and Harpoon missiles for attacking surface targets, USS *Guittaro*, commissioned in 1972, weighs 4,280 tonnes (4,213 tons), submerged, and has a length of 89 m (292 ft).

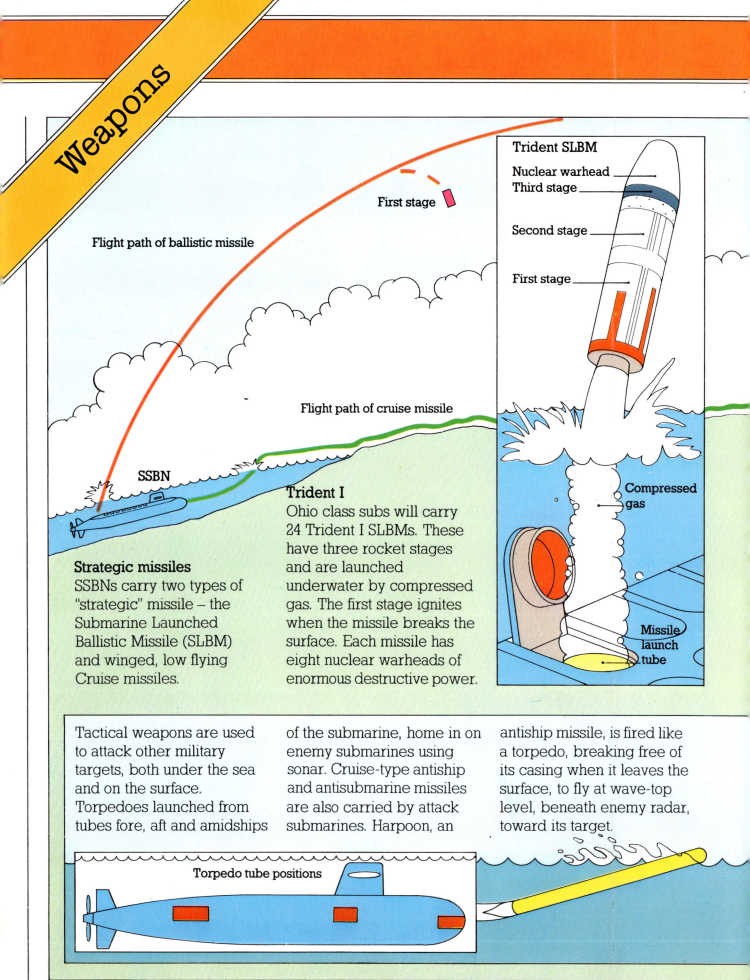

First stage

Flight path of ballistic missile

Trident SLBM
Nuclear warhead
Third stage
Second stage
First stage

Flight path of cruise missile

SSBN

Compressed gas

Missile launch tube

Strategic missiles
SSBNs carry two types of "strategic" missile – the Submarine Launched Ballistic Missile (SLBM) and winged, low flying Cruise missiles.

Trident I
Ohio class subs will carry 24 Trident I SLBMs. These have three rocket stages and are launched underwater by compressed gas. The first stage ignites when the missile breaks the surface. Each missile has eight nuclear warheads of enormous destructive power.

Tactical weapons are used to attack other military targets, both under the sea and on the surface. Torpedoes launched from tubes fore, aft and amidships of the submarine, home in on enemy submarines using sonar. Cruise-type antiship and antisubmarine missiles are also carried by attack submarines. Harpoon, an antiship missile, is fired like a torpedo, breaking free of its casing when it leaves the surface, to fly at wave-top level, beneath enemy radar, toward its target.

Torpedo tube positions

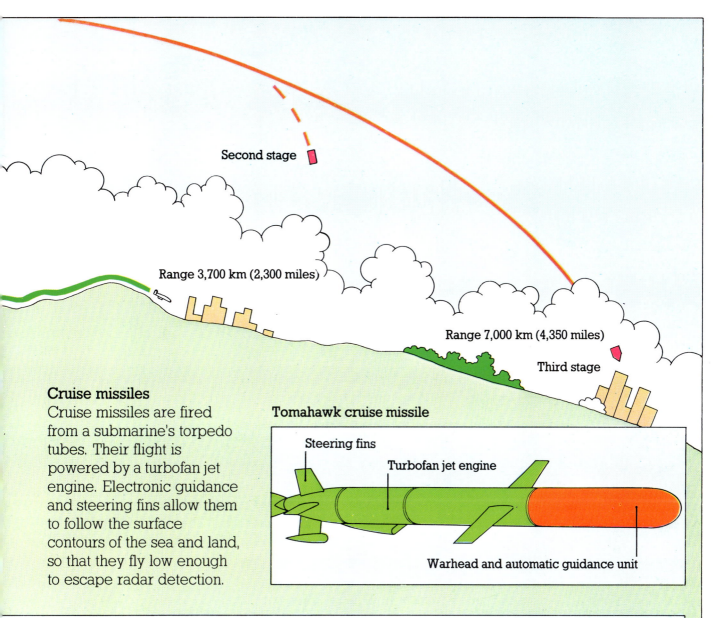

Second stage

Range 3,700 km (2,300 miles)

Range 7,000 km (4,350 miles)

Third stage

Cruise missiles

Cruise missiles are fired from a submarine's torpedo tubes. Their flight is powered by a turbofan jet engine. Electronic guidance and steering fins allow them to follow the surface contours of the sea and land, so that they fly low enough to escape radar detection.

Tomahawk cruise missile

Steering fins

Turbofan jet engine

Warhead and automatic guidance unit

Outer casing

Harpoon antiship cruise missile

Torpedo

Hunting the Killer

So effective is the threat from beneath the sea that anti-submarine warfare is one of the most important tasks of a modern navy. Antisubmarine forces combine aircraft carriers, destroyers, frigates, helicopters, long-range patrol aircraft and other submarines.

Sonar is the main tool used to find submarines, but there are many problems involved. A submarine that suspects it is being hunted will go on "silent stations" for days at a time, a stiff test for the nerves and endurance of its crew. A modern submarine can remain ultraquiet – so much so that the sound of a spoon dropped against its metal hull would be a serious breaking of silence.

The nature of the sea itself helps a submarine hide. Thermoclines, irregularities of the seabed, and even the presence of a shoal of fish can help mask a submarine's position. All of these distort the sound signals on which sonar detection depends, and antisubmarine forces may not be certain about the presence of a submarine only a few thousand meters away.

Listening devices, called hydrophones, are posted over large areas of the seabed in an attempt to provide early, long-range submarine detection. This is followed up by constant tracking, so that navies have advance warning of submarine activities. But the advantage still lies with the submarine, often unheard as well as unseen, and with the speed to outpace all surface vessels.

Hunting the enemy

Helicopters play an important role in antisubmarine warfare. This one is "dunking" a sonar buoy. If it gets a "fix" on a submarine, the helicopter has the speed to keep pace with it and can attack with depth charges. Helicopters are more maneuverable than destroyers, and can cover a wide area of ocean during a submarine hunt. The great danger for surface vessels is that the submarine will attack them before it has been detected. A group of attack submarines could easily cause havoc in this way.

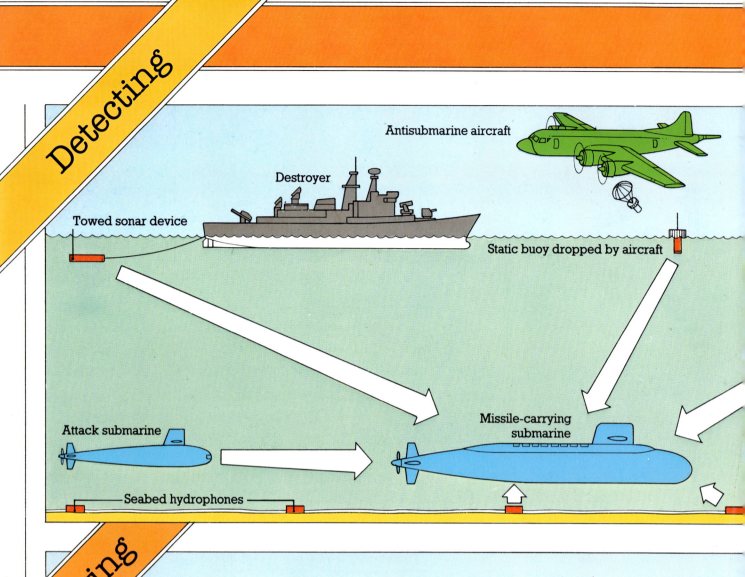

Antisubmarine aircraft

Destroyer

Towed sonar device

Static buoy dropped by aircraft

Attack submarine

Missile-carrying submarine

Seabed hydrophones

Destroyer

Attack submarine

Once a submarine has been detected and identified as an enemy, a number of weapons can be used to destroy it. The most sophisticated is the Subroc (1) missile, fired from an attack sub. This is launched like a conventional torpedo (2), but leaves the water to be guided through the air at supersonic speed. Its nuclear warhead then plunges back into the sea, to explode at, or near, its target. An explosion within about 8 km (5 miles) of the enemy sub is lethal. Subroc has a range of 55 km (34 miles). Another long-range antisubmarine weapon is the Ikara (3), a small radio-controlled aircraft launched from surface ships. Ikara releases a homing torpedo when over its target. Depth charges which explode at pre-set

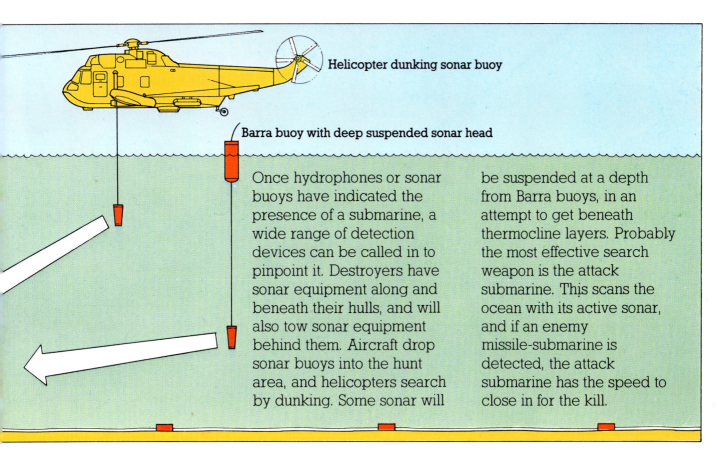

Helicopter dunking sonar buoy

Barra buoy with deep suspended sonar head

Once hydrophones or sonar buoys have indicated the presence of a submarine, a wide range of detection devices can be called in to pinpoint it. Destroyers have sonar equipment along and beneath their hulls, and will also tow sonar equipment behind them. Aircraft drop sonar buoys into the hunt area, and helicopters search by dunking. Some sonar will be suspended at a depth from Barra buoys, in an attempt to get beneath thermocline layers. Probably the most effective search weapon is the attack submarine. This scans the ocean with its active sonar, and if an enemy missile-submarine is detected, the attack submarine has the speed to close in for the kill.

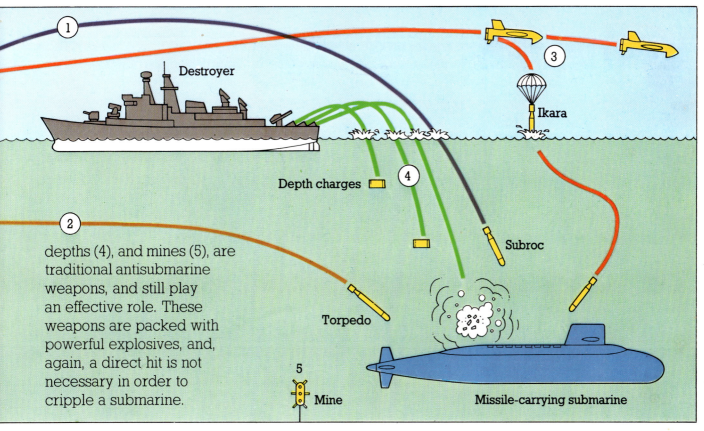

1

Destroyer

3

Ikara

Depth charges

4

2

Subroc

depths (4), and mines (5), are traditional antisubmarine weapons, and still play an effective role. These weapons are packed with powerful explosives, and, again, a direct hit is not necessary in order to cripple a submarine.

Torpedo

5

Mine

Missile-carrying submarine

Global Surveillance

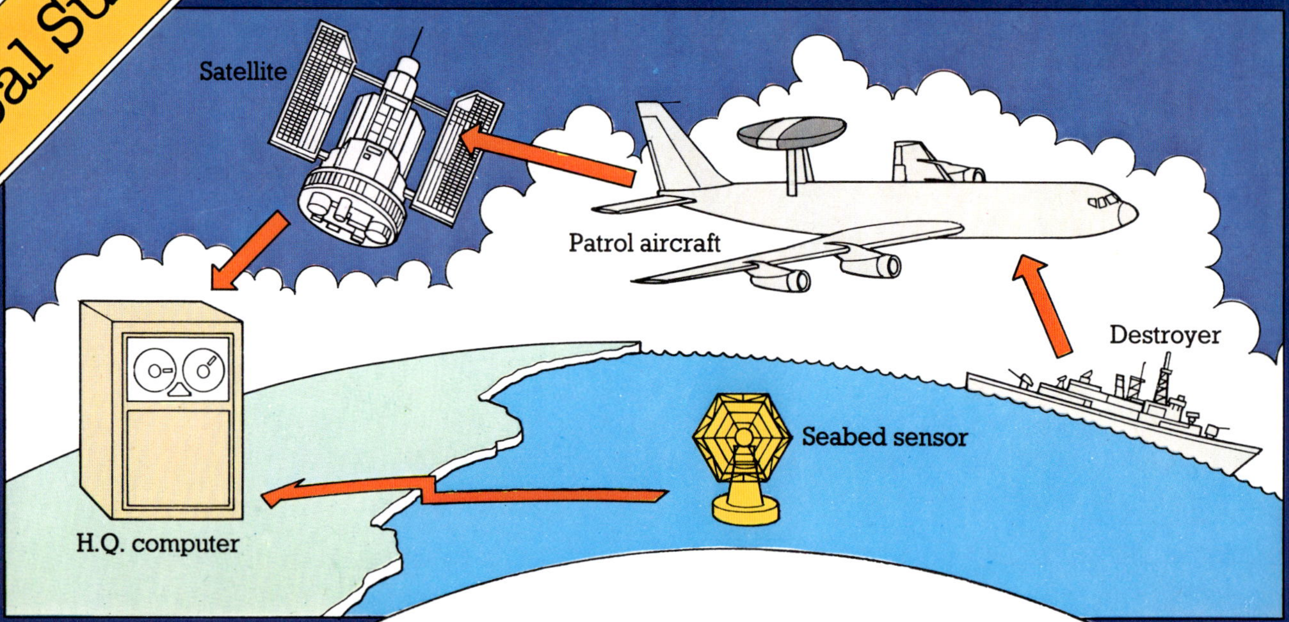
Satellite
Patrol aircraft
Destroyer
Seabed sensor
H.Q. computer

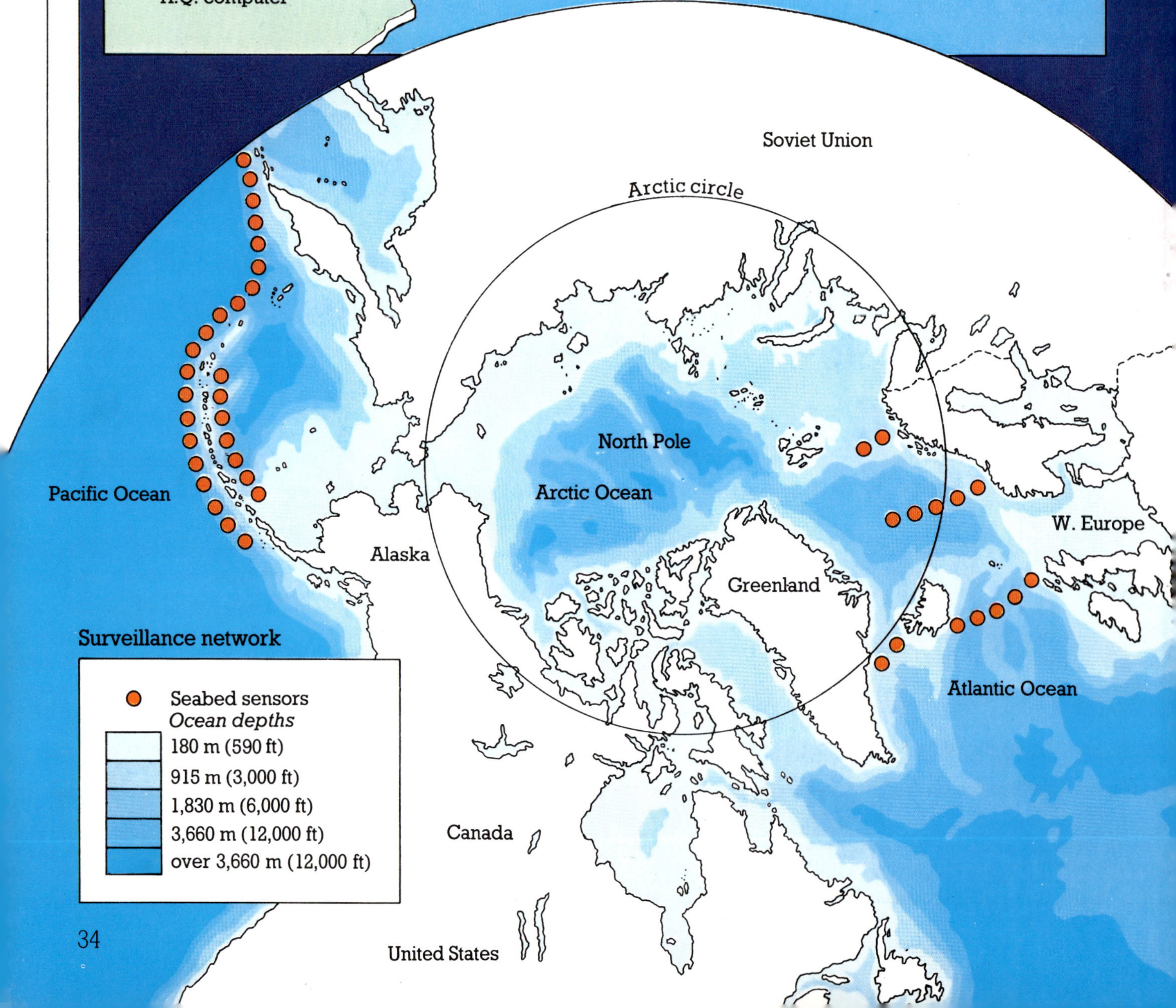
Soviet Union
Arctic circle
North Pole
Arctic Ocean
Pacific Ocean
Alaska
Greenland
W. Europe
Atlantic Ocean
Canada
United States
Surveillance network
Seabed sensors
Ocean depths
180 m (590 ft)
915 m (3,000 ft)
1,830 m (6,000 ft)
3,660 m (12,000 ft)
over 3,660 m (12,000 ft)

The threat of nuclear submarines has brought the oceans of the world under constant surveillance. Hydrophones spread over thousands of kilometers of the ocean floor are linked to shore-based computers, to monitor the movement of submarines in strategically important areas, such as the entries and exits between the Arctic and North Atlantic Oceans. Similarly, traffic into the Mediterranean and Pacific Oceans is charted. The computers are able to tell what type of submarine has been detected and build up patterns of typical submarine patrols. They are fed additional information from patrolling destroyers, long-range surveillance aircraft, and from spy satellites orbiting the Earth.

Detection of submarines underwater is likely to remain a difficult business for the time being. As detection devices become more sophisticated, so will the methods that submarines use to avoid them. Advances in submarine design and technology will lead to vessels capable of hiding at even greater depths. The ocean itself, with its uneven floor, varying thermoclines, and animal life, places a limit on the effectiveness of sound detection methods. But new detection methods may alter the balance. One system being tested now uses a special type of laser that can "see" through water, and may, at last, reveal the hidden submarine.

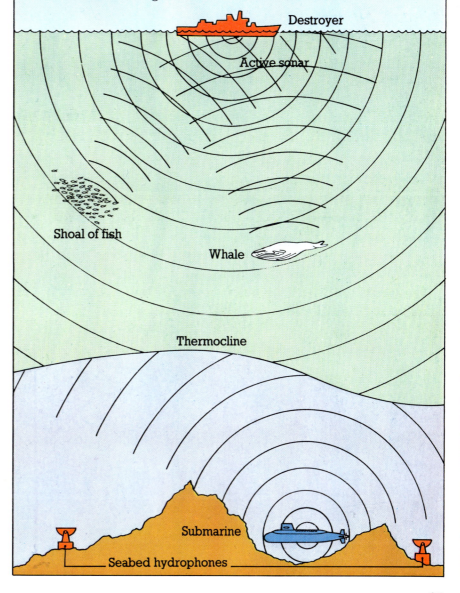

Destroyer
Active sonar
Shoal of fish
Whale
Thermocline
Submarine
Seabed hydrophones

Glossary

Ballistic missile
A missile that follows a high, curving flight path, leaving the Earth's atmosphere and then plunging down onto its target.

Commissioning
The entry of a submarine into active service for its country's navy.

Cruise missile
A winged missile that is usually powered by some form of jet engine. Advanced electronic guidance units enable cruise missiles to fly very low, avoiding enemy radar detection point.

Depth charge
An explosive device used to attack submarines. Depth charges can be set to explode at different depths.

Diesel-electric engine
The traditional submarine engine before the advent of nuclear power. Many diesel-electric subs are still in useful service. Steam generated by burning diesel fuel is used to power turbines. The turbine drives an electric motor which drives the propeller.

Fission
The splitting of atoms to generate energy. Atoms which undergo this process become radioactive, because radiation is also given off.

Harpoon
A sea-skimming missile that can be fired from both submarines and surface ships.

High frequency radio waves
The frequency of a wave measures how many complete waves there are each second. This can be many thousands in the case of high frequency radio.

Hydrophones
Microphones that pick up underwater sounds and convert them into electrical impulses for transmission.

Ikara
A radio-controlled craft which carries a torpedo, used in antisubmarine warfare.

Laser
A laser is a highly concentrated beam of light. The laser referred to in the text is of a greenish-yellow color, and it can pass through the water relatively unhindered, but the system still has a long way to go before it becomes operational.

Mine
An underwater explosive, usually moored to the seabed at a certain depth in areas of known submarine activity.

Neutron
An electrically neutral particle in the nucleus of an atom.

Snorkel
A device used by diesel-electric submarines. It is raised above the surface to take in air to feed the diesel engine.

Sonar signature
The distinctive sound made by a submarine or surface ship. Each different type of ship or submarine has its own distinctive sonar signature.

SSBN
The abbreviation used for missile-carrying submarines. It stands for the rather back-to-front phrase, "Submarines, Ballistic missile, Nuclear."

Strategic weapons
These are long-range nuclear weapons. They are aimed at civilian and military targets, and the threat to use them is intended to prevent the outbreak of a nuclear war.

Subroc
A submarine-launched nuclear missile, designed to destroy other submarines.

Thermocline
A layer in the ocean where warmer surface water meets the colder water of deep ocean. This layer can reflect and distort underwater sound waves.

Trident
One of the latest submarine-launched ballistic missiles. It has a much greater range than previous ballistic missiles.

Turbofan engine
The type of jet engine used in many cruise missiles. It has automatic air intake, and is less noisy than other types of jet.

Very Low Frequency Radio Waves (VLF)
A radio transmission that can penetrate seawater to a limited extent. Extremely low frequency (ELF) radio waves are also used to communicate with submarines, but this system requires highly complex and expensive transmission equipment.

Index

Aladdin Books would like to thank the following for their valuable help in the production of this book:

Sippican Corporation (Ocean Systems Division), Rockwell International (Autonetics Marine Systems Division), Ferranti Computer Systems, the Royal Navy (U.K.), Vickers Shipbuilding Group Ltd., The American Society of Naval Engineers Inc., Military Archive and Research Services, the U.S. Navy, Ministry of Defence (U.K.), Rolls Royce and Associates, and the General Dynamics Corporation.

Front endpapers: The launch of HMS *Trafalgar*, 1982 (Vickers Shipbuilding and Engineering Ltd), *back endpapers:* Breaking the polar ice (Military Archive and Research Services)